WORDS

Essays on Writing, Reading, and Life

JESSICA MCCANN

Perspective Books

Perspective Books
Phoenix, Arizona USA

www.JessicaMcCann.com

Portions of this work were adapted from essays/articles that originally appeared in other mediums including, but not limited to: Greatthoughts.com, TheMillions.com, Booksbywomen.org, Readlearnwrite.com, *ASU Research Magazine,* and *The Writer Magazine*

Cover photo: Richard Villalon
Interior book graphics: the8monkey
Author photo: Mike McCann

Words: Essays on Writing, Reading, and Life – 1st ed.
Trade Paperback: ISBN 978-0-9994602-4-5
E-book: ISBN 978-0-9994602-5-2

About the Author

 **Jessica McCann** is an award-winning historical novelist and has worked as a professional freelance writer and editor for magazines, universities, corporations, and nonprofits for more than thirty years. She lives with her family in Phoenix.

In *WORDS*, she has woven together a collection of personal essays and writing tips that offer a unique glimpse into her writing journey and process. McCann shares her passion for books, as well as research that shows how reading improves our lives. With a philosophy that is equally pragmatic and optimistic, *WORDS* will appeal to readers and writers alike.

Historical Novels by Jessica McCann
All Different Kinds of Free
Peculiar Savage Beauty

Connect with the author at
www.JessicaMcCann.com

> "A book is a box of words,
> until you open it."
> – Ursula K. Le Guin, American author

Contents

Contents

Introduction

"To write is to live on the edge
of the beautiful wilderness."
– Laura Munson, memoirist and novelist

It's impossible to boil down why I write to one
event or experience. From my earliest foggy
memories, it's clear I've always been drawn to books
and words – compelled to gather them, driven to
string them together. Some people collect Hummels.
Others knit scarves. I collect prose and knit
sentences.

My writing life (my entire life) has evolved from
hundreds, perhaps thousands, of reading- and writing-

related experiences. I remember the regular library trips with my parents as a little girl. I embrace the epiphany of parallelism, learned from my senior high school English teacher. There have been countless books read and absorbed, from *The Velveteen Rabbit* and *Winnie the Pooh* to *The Liar's Club* and *The Invisible Mountain*. As a journalist, I have interviewed dozens of people who enlightened and intrigued me — neurosurgeons, custodians, CEOs, teachers, politicians, garbage truck drivers, Black Jack dealers and more. As a novelist, I have researched historical events and probed the human psyche. My office files are stuffed with snippets of prose, inspiring statements and beautifully constructed paragraphs written by novices and icons alike. My bookshelves overflow.

Collectively, this is why I write — to reflect on and make sense of all that I've learned and loved and experienced. I share my writing because I believe every one of us endeavors to make sense of it all.

Through reading and writing, we learn from one another.

And so, within the following pages, I humbly offer observations and reflections on my writing journey and process, and of my life-long love affair with books.

Trusting Instinct

> "A curious mind probing for truth
> may well set your scribbling ass free."
> – Mary Karr, *The Art of Memoir*

How does one become a writer? It requires only a single action. To write.

How does one become published, or earn money as a writer? That's another matter. Earn a college degree, work up the ladder in the publishing business, or get a job in academia. These are the fairly direct, standard conventions. Still, as with any ambition, the path you ultimately take to reach the desired outcome is uniquely yours.

My path has been twisty and unconventional.

There's a drawer in my office containing writing samples I've never sent out with query letters or shown to potential clients. Hidden under a stack of recycled manila folders are books I crafted in grade school, stories I wrote in junior high, and articles I penned for my high school newspaper. Once in a while, when I'm rearranging the office or doing a little spring cleaning, I rediscover them. Every time I look through them, they remind me that – although I've had my share of self-doubt and detours along my career path – I have always been a writer.

Throughout school, I was the kid whose heart raced with delight when the teacher announced a book report or persuasive essay, while my classmates moaned and broke out in a collective cold sweat. I didn't necessarily dream of being "a writer." It was just something I enjoyed. I loved putting words to paper, playing with them, moving this one here and that one there, replacing yet another with something better – like assembling a black and white jigsaw puzzle.

My working life began at fifteen, waiting tables evenings and weekends.

At seventeen, I landed a job in the produce department at Smitty's, a locally-owned grocery store. It was hard work, which the compensation reflected. My hourly pay was more than three times the minimum wage in those days. It was a good job, and I adored my bosses and coworkers. Smitty's treated its employees well; many worked there for decades. At the time, I saw no reason to aspire to anything else.

Attending college was never on the radar. My parents didn't talk about it, and I knew we didn't have the money for it. My grades weren't good enough to land a scholarship, and I refused to go into debt. Besides, the only things I loved doing and would have wanted to pursue in college were dancing and writing. Actually earning a living in either vocation was a fantasy that couldn't be entertained.

At eighteen, I would graduate high school and move into an apartment on my own. My life goals were to keep a roof over my head and food in my belly. A career at Smitty's would have accomplished those goals.

That mindset shifted during the last few months of high school, thanks to my newspaper class teacher and a unique opportunity offered by St. Joseph's Hospital and Medical Center in Phoenix.

The hospital hosted an annual Young Reporters Press Conference (back in the day when health care institutions had generous "community relations" budgets). Essentially, a panel of surgeons would line up in a mock press-conference and spout all sorts of technical jargon about the latest medical breakthrough, while several dozen high school kids scrawled feverishly in their spiral notebooks. This was followed by a tour of the hospital and a free lunch.

My newspaper teacher asked our class who would be interested in attending the press conference and three of us raised our hands. There were two slots available. The only fair way to decide who could go was to draw straws. I lost, which no longer seemed fair. So I pulled my teacher aside later and asked what she thought the hospital folks would do if I went anyway, just in case there were any last minute no-shows. She had no idea, she said, but would love to find out and so gave me her blessing to take the day off school.

A day off school and a free lunch.

Of course everybody showed.

Luckily, the media relations woman was impressed by my initiative and made room for me. Later in the day, I thumbed through the press kit I'd been given. In it was a Xeroxed flyer soliciting volunteers to write small articles for the hospital's employee newsletter. It sounded interesting. I started volunteering four hours a week, all I could manage in addition to school and my part-time job. Within a few weeks, she asked what it would take for me to put in more hours at the hospital.

"You'd need to start paying me," I said with unabashed seventeen-year-old candor.

So, she did – four bucks an hour.

Thus began my freelance writing adventures. I graduated from high school a few months later and increased my hours at the hospital. I interviewed employees who had worked in the hospital's laundry facilities for thirty years and neurologists who had saved the lives of world dignitaries. I donned medical scrubs to observe new surgical techniques and furry animal costumes to help educate school children about water and bicycle safety. I wrote dozens of articles about the people I had met and the things I had learned. I was hooked.

The hospital's communications department consisted of an amazing group of women who took me under their collective wing. Each mentored me in their respective areas – external communications, media relations, community outreach, and employee communications. They exposed me to a myriad of business and journalistic writing styles and approaches. That became my formal education in the writing profession.

Word spread of my enthusiasm and rock-bottom rates, and referrals soon led to writing assignments for other organizations.

At the age of twenty, I married my soul mate; at twenty-three, I gave birth to our first child.

During that formative decade, I had already begun to feel the impact of years working long shifts on cement floors in the produce department. Wearing support-hose only slowed the development of varicose veins. Dr. Scholl's shoe inserts merely postponed the need to ice my knees after work. At the same time, I worried about whether freelancing full-time was viable, whether it would help pay the mortgage and feed my family.

These thoughts prompted me to seek out a "real" job in communications or publishing. I ended up working in salaried positions as a communications coordinator, a magazine editor, and a book editor. All good jobs. There were many benefits to being employed full-time, but the freedom, latitude, and learning that came from freelancing kept calling me back. After the birth of my second child – roughly ten years after my first assignment at St. Joe's – I made the decision to focus full-time on freelance writing. And I never looked back.

> "It is impossible to discourage the real writers; they don't give a damn what you say, they're going to write."
> – Sinclair Lewis, American novelist

Reading and writing stories comprise some of my earliest memories. Yet, fiction writing didn't have a role in my professional career until my late-thirties. The desire to make up stories had been put on ice in the eighth grade. I had turned in a short-story assignment, and my English teacher gave me a D. He said the story was unimaginative, the ending a cliché, the writing lazy. Thirteen is a tender age, and I was crushed.

Maybe his assessment was accurate. Maybe he was hoping to fire me up and get me to work harder to prove him wrong. Maybe he was a big, mean jerk whose own dreams of being a writer had been crushed by someone else long before. Who knows? All I know for sure is that he trampled my confidence. I had zero desire to write fiction and face such criticism ever again.

I focused instead on nonfiction and built a successful career as a business writer and journalist. My stable of regular clients ranged from universities and nonprofit organizations to casinos and international corporations. Assignments ran the gamut from articles, brochures, and ghostwritten speeches to websites, newsletters, and annual reports.

Once you venture down a certain path, especially when the sun shines brightly upon that path, it's pretty hard to find the motivation and courage to wander off into the dark scary woods in search of something different. Thus, I stayed with what I knew I could do well, stayed with what was safe.

But safe gets boring after a while.

Much as I enjoy writing for a living, maintaining a freelance business can be tedious work that often includes a whole lot of not writing (networking and client meetings, invoicing and bill collecting, scheduling and proofreading.). About the time I hit my five-year anniversary of full-time freelancing, I began to question whether I was still "a writer" or simply an entrepreneur who could successfully string together words. I was bored writing what felt like the same-old things month after month, year after year. My clients still seemed happy with my work, but there was a cloud hanging over me. I felt stifled creatively, felt I was doing my clients a disservice, and felt it would soon catch up to me in a bad way.

I swore I would never let freelancing become my own version of the nine-to-five grind, nor let the business of writing dampen my joy of writing.

So I began using creative writing prompts to draft short stories. The goal was never to publish those stories, or even to ever let anyone read them. I just needed to shake things up, to flex my creative muscles and exercise a different part of my brain. Within a short amount of time, a few amazing things happened. One, I began to understand that good fiction writing isn't a whole heck of a lot different than good nonfiction; two, I dared to believe the stories I was writing weren't half bad; and three, I remembered how much I loved writing just for fun.

One Saturday morning, I sat at the kitchen table with my HP Mini®, fingers flying at the keyboard. A cup of creamy coffee and a scribbled-up notepad sat to my right, a paperback novel to my left.

"Whatcha working on?" my teenage daughter asked on her way to the fridge.

"I'm writing a review for this book I just read."

My daughter stopped and swiveled around, a look of bewilderment on her lovely face. "Voluntarily?"

"Yep!" I said with a giggle and a nod, before taking a sip of my coffee and returning to the keys.

My brain was clicking again.

Perhaps inevitably, the idea of a novel started forming in my mind. Then it started forming in a computer document. In its earliest stages, I never believed the novel would ever get published (hoped, perhaps, but not believed). It was just a story I felt compelled to write, and I was enjoying the creative process.

On a whim (and with the hope of winning a few bucks), I entered the first chapters in a few writing competitions as a novel-in-progress. I didn't win, but I received semi-finalist recognition in two respected contests. That's when I first started to believe I might have the chops to actually write a novel that people would want to read.

When the manuscript for *All Different Kinds of Free* won the Freedom in Fiction Prize, publishing a novel was no longer a crazy dream. It became a tangible goal that I wrote into my business plan.

I'm fortunate to have figured out how to be "a writer" on so many levels, and to have married a man who always encourages me to do so. Some days I'm editing articles for a client newsletter. Other days I'm crafting scenes for my next novel. And on the occasional Saturday morning, I may even write a book review "voluntarily," simply because I loved the story. Deep down, I guess I'll always be that kid whose heart races with delight at putting words on the page.

Opening Boxes

"Those who don't believe in magic will
never find it."
– Roald Dahl, British novelist

Long before Hermione Granger mesmerized little
girls with her cleverness and magic, a young witch
who lost her broom right before Halloween captured
my heart. Jeanne Massey's *The Littlest Witch* is the first
book I recall reading entirely by myself. I was in
second grade.

My family had just returned from a trip to the
public library, and I promptly disappeared into my
bedroom with an armload of books. I'm sure I read
them all. But there was something about *The Littlest
Witch* that gripped me. I adored it.

For days after, I plotted and schemed to come up a way to keep the book, rather than take it back to the library. Alas, when the due date arrived, my mom made sure all the books were promptly returned. I consoled myself with the thought that by returning it, some other little girl would get to enjoy it, too. It was an epiphany. Books are meant to be shared.

Fast forward thirty-plus years. My debut novel had just been published, and I was making the rounds to local bookstores with review copies in hand. I was wearing my metaphorical marketing hat, trying to sell books. The Arizona State University bookstore was among the places I visited, since I had done a lot of freelance writing for the university through the years. I was on campus around lunch time, so I grabbed some food at the Memorial Union and found a shady place outside to eat and people-watch.

The MU was a swarm of students and faculty – texting, typing on laptops, talking on cell phones. They all seemed so busy, so plugged in. All I could think was what a perfect day it was to sit in under a tree and read a book. My marketing hat had apparently blown away on the spring breeze, and my reader hat magically appeared in its place. But the only book I had with me was my own.

That's when my second-grade epiphany echoed in my head. *Books are meant to be shared.*

I pulled out one of the review copies from my bag, opened it to the inside cover and wrote a note: "Books are meant to be shared. Please read this, if you'd like, and then leave it somewhere for someone else to enjoy." I gathered my things, set the book down on the bench beside me and walked away.

Since then I've left behind many more books in public places (books I had read and wanted to share, as well as own books). It's just plain fun to do. In my mind's eye, I picture someone accidentally sitting on a book. He picks it up, perplexed, then cracks open the cover and gets swept away by the story. Now that's magic.

> "I cannot remember the books I've read any
> more than the meals I have eaten; even so,
> they have made me."
> – Ralph Waldo Emerson, American poet

Books are intoxicating, from the smell of the paper
and ink to the feel of the binding and pages. I love
how they look lined neatly on a shelf or stacked
haphazardly around the room. I love what a collection
of books reveals about its owner. It amazes me that
one-hundred-thousand or so words can coalesce
between the covers of one volume and relay a story
with the potential to change lives.

Beyond the pure magic and aesthetics, books make
us who we are, just as Emerson said. Much research
has been done on the benefits of reading books –
novels in particular. The consensus of the data is that
reading helps us to be smarter, happier, even nicer.

A meta-analysis research project, led by University
of Rochester Psychologist David Dodell-Feder,
reviewed fourteen studies on the relationship between

reading fiction and empathy. The researchers concluded that, compared to reading non-fiction or not reading at all, reading fiction produced a "small, statistically significant improvement in social-cognitive performance."

Research also found that the more literary the book, the better the results. Freelance writer Jessica Stillman reported on the data in a piece for Inc.com.[1] Some of the high-profile studies analyzed had test subjects read either "pulpy" books or serious works of fiction, and then tested their ability to perceive others' emotions. Other studies, she explained, asked people how many famous literary writers they recognized before giving them similar reading tests. Both approaches found that exposure to literature boosts emotional intelligence quotient (EQ).

"In short, the sum total of science on the subject says reading fiction really will make you a little nicer and more empathetic," Stillman wrote.

Eastern Kentucky University Professor Michael Austin explained why in a piece for *Psychology Today*, titled "Want a Better Life? Read a Book."[2]

"Acquiring a deeper understanding about ourselves and the world we live in and applying it to life is conducive to building a better life and a better world," Austin wrote. One of the best ways to do this, he asserted, is by reading a book that engages the mind and inspires conversation. Austin referred to Mortimer Adler's 1940s classic, *How to Read a Book*, and highlighted the following excerpt:

> "A good book can teach you about the world and about yourself. … You become wiser. Not just more knowledgeable – books that provide nothing but information can produce that result. But wiser, in the sense that you are more deeply aware of the great and enduring truths of human life."

I couldn't agree more. If working freelance at St. Joe's Hospital was my formal education in the profession of writing, then reading novels has been my formal education in psychology, anthropology, and the humanities.

> "A book is a friend.
> You can never have too many."
> — Gary Paulsen, American author

When I was in the fourth grade, a couple of the moms made several visits to our class to teach us "life skills." They addressed topics like how to make new friends, to be kind to others, and so on. During one visit they announced that the final week would include a cupcake party, and we were each to place an advance order so they would know how many to bake. Most kids ordered chocolate. A handful of us ordered vanilla, and we were promptly derided. That's boring, the chocolate-eaters said. Vanilla isn't even a real flavor.

The next week, the moms arrived bearing their tasty treats. The vanilla cupcakes had whipped cream frosting and rainbow sprinkles. The chocolate cupcakes were plain. And the rumblings soon began. What? No fair! How come you got frosting? Trade with me.

No trades, we vanilla-eaters gloated. That's what you get for ordering stupid-old chocolate. We have frosting, and you don't.

The adults let us grumble and gloat for a bit, then put an end to it. Quiet down and eat your cupcakes, they said. So we did. And a funny thing happened. The chocolate-eaters soon discovered a delicious surprise. The moms had baked M&M candies into the bottoms of their cupcakes. A rich, colorful, chocolate bonus. Huzzah! Chocolate was the best choice after all, or so the complainers said.

That's when the moms explained their little experiment to us. Explained how important it is to be grateful for what we receive, even when we might feel someone else has something better. Explained that sometimes, even when life seems most unfair, we could discover something unexpected, something wonderful, something better than what we thought we wanted.

Blah, blah, blah.

At the time, the message was lost on us kids. We mostly felt manipulated, used, a bit like lab rats. Yet, their lesson seeped into my subconscious and stayed with me. They were right, of course. It's not always easy advice to follow, but they were 100 percent spot on.

As adults, too often, we're not a whole lot more mature than that group of fourth graders – criticizing, judging, and teasing others for their choices. I often experience this phenomenon during discussions about books. People are quick to condemn others' reading preferences. You like literary fiction? That's so boring. Oh, you read romance. Those books are trashy. Is that sci-fi? Why waste your time reading about something that could never really happen?

Why can't we just say, "Hey! I'm a reader, too. How are you enjoying that book?"

With the explosion of e-books and print-on-demand publishing technology, books have become much more accessible than they once were. There are literally millions of books out there. Far too many for one person to ever read. So why not celebrate the variety? Maybe that so-called boring literary novel, if you take the time to savor it, just might have a delicious, satisfying surprise in the end. And perhaps the romance novel that seems to be all whipped cream and sprinkles just might nourish your need for a happy ending.

Those of us who write for a living, or aspire to, would be especially wise to heed this advice.

For one thing, reading a wide range of genres expands our minds, introduces us to new ideas and teaches us about good writing (or, sometimes, about not-so-good writing, but that's also a beneficial thing). A voracious reading appetite just might lead us to discover something unexpected, something

wonderful, something better than what we thought
we wanted from a book. That makes us stronger
writers.

For another thing, having respect for all kinds of
readers empowers us to break barriers and attract fans
to our stories that we might not have anticipated. My
debut historical novel, for example, was marketed as
women's fiction. Yet, I've received many thoughtful
reviews from male readers who were moved by the
book's multiple perspectives on slavery and freedom,
and its universal themes of self-reliance, perseverance,
and hope.

It's just like those bakeries that have sprung up all
over the place that serve only cupcakes. You know
the ones. Dozens of flavors and combinations. Red
velvet, pumpkin, peanut butter chocolate, lemon-
ginger, you name it. It blows my fourth-grade mind.

Eat whatever cupcake you want, and read
whatever book you like. Don't judge others for their
choices. And don't be afraid to sample something
different once in a while. Have a chai latte cupcake

with your historical fiction, or try a rocky road cupcake with your paranormal thriller. It's all good.

> "Listen, and you will realize that we are made not from cells or from atoms. We are made from stories."
> – Mia Couto, Mozambican writer

Writers love to talk about *voice*. We're obsessed with it, frankly. It's a key element of any written work and, arguably, the most important element of fiction. Authors seem to speak of it in the most earnest and whimsical ways, too.

"I write only because there is a voice within me that will not be still," poet Sylvia Plath wrote.

Science-fiction writer Ray Bradbury once mused, "I wake early and hear my morning voices leaping around in my head like jumping beans. I get out of bed to trap them before they escape."

Voice also refers to writing style. It's the words authors choose, the way they strings those words together, how they say what it is they want to say, that creates voice.

When a novel is produced as an audio book, this literary term gains a more explicit meaning – it becomes an actual voice. How does it feel for a novelist the first time you hear your writing being read aloud by someone else? For me, it was disorienting and a little weird.

My publisher had contracted a professional voice artist to read my debut historical novel as an audio book and, of course, I was thrilled. Yet, when I listened to the first sample, it was strange to hear my main character speaking to me in a voice that was different from the one I had been hearing in my head.

The novel, *All Different Kinds of Free*, was inspired by a true story, and I had worked hard to create an authentic voice for the main character and narrator, Margaret Morgan. An educated, free woman of color in the 1830s, Margaret was kidnapped, along with her children, to be sold into slavery. Labeled as a runaway slave, she fought against all odds to prove and regain her freedom. My goal was for her voice to be both strong and vulnerable, equally wise and naive, sometimes despondent and yet always hopeful.

I had read the complete manuscript maybe a dozen times as it went through the many phases of revision, copyediting, and proofreading that led up to publication. A couple times, I even read it out loud. It had a certain cadence in my mind, a certain timbre and tone.

It's not that the voice artist had done a poor job of reading it. On the contrary, Mia Bankston's portrayal of Margaret was expert – warm and endearing, at times gripping and heartbreaking. Still, it wasn't exactly the voice I had come to know in the roughly ten years it took to research, write and publish my book.

The shock of listening to that first audio sample was similar to the shock of receiving the first round of serious edits on a manuscript. It's a punch to the gut. Sure, you're expecting it. You think you're ready for it. But when the blow lands, it still knocks the wind out of you.

From what I've read, it's not unlike the feelings experienced when novels are optioned for film. I've read a handful of author interviews about book-movie deals. Most were cautionary tales about how much your book may change – characters may be added, plot twists removed or entire endings rewritten. It makes sense. Film is a different medium with different rules.

With an audio book, however, the voice artist reads the novel exactly how it is written. Every contraction stays put, every comma in its place. Nothing changes. Yet, somehow, it's still different. My initial email to Bankston was professional, something like, "Thanks for sending the sample. Can't wait to listen to it. I'll let you know next week if I have any feedback." Even as I clicked on the send button, my stomach was in knots. Would I be able to provide constructive, rational feedback?

I let a day or two pass. I tried to occupy my mind with other projects, while I nursed my literary laryngitis. Then I gave myself the same advice I always do when I'm feeling the sting of edits or the weight of a tough project. *Get over yourself, Jessica.* I took off my spiffy, new yippee-I'm-a-published-author hat and put on my weathered professional-freelance-writer-and-editor hat. And I listened to the audio file again with fresh, objective ears.

I paused the recording at times, jotting down general thoughts and noting places where the pace felt a little fast, where certain phrases or words needed more or less emphasis, and when I felt the voice artist hit a comfortable stride. Bankston had an expert way of changing her voice to reflect different characters in dialogue. There was also a sincerity in her narration, a quality that made Margaret feel genuine and alive. The more I listened, the more comfortable I became with Margaret's new voice and the way Bankston brought her to life.

Bankston and I corresponded a handful of times. I shared my feedback, and she listened to it. She shared her thoughts, and I was impressed by her professionalism. Several days later, she sent an edited recording of the original sample. It was perfect. At that point, Bankston set about the task of recording the entire book, and I plunged back into my own work.

Still, the idea of voice nagged at me. Writers aren't the only ones obsessed with it, after all. I challenge you to find any interviews with editors or agents that don't include some sort of quote about their desire to discover an author with *a distinctive voice*. What does that mean, anyway?

"By voice, I think they mean not only a unique way of putting words together, but a unique sensibility, a distinctive way of looking at the world, an outlook that enriches an author's oeuvre," wrote literary agent Donald Maass in his book *Writing the Breakout Novel*.[3]

Bestselling author John Grisham frames it in broader terms: "In life, finding a voice is speaking and living the truth. Each of you is an original. Each of you has a distinctive voice. When you find it, your story will be told."

Ah, yes, the story. Voice empowers story. And isn't that the most critical element in all writing?

How many books have you read in which the writing, the language, the voice all dazzled you, and yet the story itself somehow fell flat? The books that stay with me the longest are, in fact, the ones that have both a distinctive voice and a compelling story.

"Writing isn't just on the page," asserted Donna Jo Napoli, a prolific children's and young-adult author. "It's voices in the reader's head."

In the case of audio books, it's also a voice in the reader's ears – the voice that tells the story in its distinctive way.

Knitting Prose

> "Words are as beautiful as wild horses, and
> sometimes as difficult to corral."
> – Ted Berkman, author and journalist

Composing short stories helped me breathe life
back into my writing. My once-sedentary creativity
got a fresh burst of energy from the regular exercise. I
was pleased with the results. My clients were pleased.
Fine. Great. Mission accomplished. Yet, that wasn't
the end of the story, rather the beginning of a whole
new one. My renewed love of writing fiction
compelled me to alter my entire career trajectory. The
new goal was to earn my living as a novelist.

The more I read and studied and wrote, the more I
learned that my experience as a nonfiction writer and

my goal to become a fiction writer complemented each other. Being efficient with the language, using vivid imagery, and telling a compelling story are universal to good writing, regardless of the genre. And, the research and organization skills I'd honed as a journalist would come in handy when developing and writing novels.

"Like any work, fiction writing requires preparation, planning, discipline and drive," stressed David Fryxell in his book *Writing Fast (While Writing Well)*.[4] "The fiction writer must focus his efforts long before the first word hits the page."

Finding Your Process

All good writing takes time and effort, though the process one goes through for different types of writing can be unique. Author Bruce Holland Rogers has written both commercial and literary fiction. He addresses their differences in an unbiased way, in his nonfiction book, *Word Work: Surviving and Thriving as a Writer*.[5]

In a nutshell, the more a book is action-adventure
or plot-driven, the better it lends itself to what he calls
the pressure-cooker approach to writing – that is the
nose-to-the-grindstone, get the draft down on paper,
write fast approach. The more literary the book,
however, the slower it must be cooked up. He
describes his "slow-cooking technique" as somewhat
nebulous. What does he spend his time on?

> "I'm writing character sketches. I'm writing
> biographies about my characters, covering
> mundane details like what they look like, but
> also psychological details about how they
> perceive and act in the world. ... I'm reading
> [about the elements and themes of the book,
> such as father-son relationships, steam
> locomotives, and manic depression]. And I'm
> writing about the meaning of these things,
> little essays to myself about what a steam
> locomotive tells me about the universe, about
> human beings. ... I wrote many pages about

[the book] before I was able to type
CHAPTER ONE....

Not everything I'm doing at this stage
looks even remotely like work. I'm walking
and thinking about my novel, listening to
music while I daydream about the novel.

The trick lies in knowing when to shift
gears and produce scenes, when to stop and
noodle some more."

Holland Rogers' analogy of pressure-cooker versus
slow-cooker resonates with me on multiple levels.
Slow-cookers have always delighted me. A hodge-
podge of meat, vegetables, and whatnot gets tossed in
the Crock-Pot® in the morning. The ingredients
simmer together all day. Their flavors blend. Their
aromas comingle and fill the house with the tang of
possibility. Come dinner time, the medley has been
transformed into a savory meal that brings the whole
family to the table with anticipation. I love cooking
this way.

My novel writing is also slow-cooked. A hodge-podge of ideas, research, themes, and characters get thrown into the pot in the beginning. Then they simmer together, for a very long time, before they are transformed into the rich, savory story I want them to become. Slow-cooking a novel isn't nearly as easy as slow-cooking chili, stew, or gumbo. Yet, if the mix of ingredients is right, the result can be just as fulfilling.

Not all my writing lends itself to this slow-cooking technique, just as Holland Rogers suggested. In fact, most everything else I write comes together far more quickly. As a full-time freelance writer, I've written everything from annual reports, white papers, and magazine articles to creative nonfiction, personal essays, and press releases. Each is challenging in its own right. Each takes time and thought and effort. None seem to require the slow simmer that my novels do to reach their full potential.

I believe the secret to success in writing (success in any task, really) lies in gaining an appreciation for and acceptance of the process that works best for you.

Some days I lament my agonizingly-slow process of novel writing. Part of me enjoys, even thrives on, the pressure-cooker process I utilize to write most of my freelance writing assignments. If only I could write my novels that quickly and efficiently.

Other days, I relish the slow-cooker pace of my novel writing. I'm grateful for the time it takes for the ideas to gel and for the unexpected revelations to come. It's generally worth the wait.

Certain things in life cannot be rushed. If I were to offer up my Crock-Pot meal for lunch instead of dinner, the meat might be tough, the vegetables crunchy, the broth bland. And if I were to offer up my novel-in-progress too quickly, the characters might be flat, the plot predictable, the imagery dull. Far better to let it all simmer, to ensure a rich gumbo of well-blended words and ideas that will bring the reader to the page with anticipation.

Taking Your Time

That simmer time allows opportunity for magic to happen. Once we commit to making the stew (or writing the novel) by gathering the ingredients and throwing them in the pot, the thing seems to take on a life of its own. In her seminal book, *The Artist's Way*, Julia Cameron[6] calls it the answer to a prayer, the hand of God, or perhaps the favor of the universe "activated by our own hand when we act in behalf of our truest dreams." It's a lofty idea, and it resonates with me.

In hindsight, I can see how things I didn't even know I would need (didn't even know existed) began falling into place once I truly committed – heart and soul – to writing a novel.

For example, one of books I read as research for writing Margaret Morgan's story was *Uncle Tom's Cabin* by Harriet Beecher Stowe. The novel had created a stir when it was published in 1851. Many people were stunned by the light it shed on the horrors of slavery; just as many questioned the basis of truth in the novel. Such conflicting viewpoints were something I encountered a lot in my research on slavery. It was something that lingered in my mind even when I wasn't working on the book. It was in my thoughts while I completed freelance assignments or wandered the aisles of the grocery store, even while vacationing with my family.

In the summer of 2000, my husband and I took our kids on an extended road-trip to visit family in Colorado and the Midwest. While in Iowa, a cousin took us to the Living History Farms in Urbandale. It was a lovely day and a fun activity for the little kiddos (and the big kiddos, like me, who love being immersed in history). We explored the homes, shops and businesses of its 1875 Town of Walnut Hill. As we entered the General Store, I was drawn to a shelf of books (shocking, right?). That's when *A Key to Uncle Tom's Cabin* jumped out at me. Because so many people had doubted the authenticity of her novel, Beecher Stowe gathered the facts and documents upon which the story was founded and published

them the following year. I bought the book and
devoured it. It became one of the most useful and
treasured research tools in my arsenal as I wrote *All
Different Kinds of Free.*

A Key to Uncle Tom's Cabin is a slim a book
featuring an off-white imageless cover with black text.
Had I not been writing a novel about slavery, I surely
would have overlooked it. But I was, and I didn't.
Was it mere luck? Coincidence? I believe otherwise.

"In outsized lives, such moments stand out in bas-
relief, large as Mount Rushmore: Lewis and Clark
headed west. Isak Dinesen took off for Africa,"
explained Cameron in *The Artist's Way.* "We all have
our Africas, those dark and romantic notions that call
to our deepest selves. When we answer that call, when
we commit to it, we set into motion the principle that
C.G. Jung dubbed synchronicity, loosely defined as a
fortuitous intermeshing of events. Back in the sixties,
we called it serendipity. Whatever you choose to call
it, once you begin your creative recovery you may be
startled to find it cropping up everywhere."

This serendipity doesn't just come in the form of the right research at the right time. It happens when an eclectic collection of ideas coalesce into a new idea or theme for something you've been working on for years.

Since the release of *Peculiar Savage Beauty*, many readers have asked how the idea for Woody's window dust paintings came to me. The short answer? Serendipity.

The longer answer is that it was an amalgamation of several elements that seemed to throw themselves in my writing path in the six years it took me to write the book.

Peculiar Savage Beauty is the story of a headstrong young woman who charges into the heart of the wind- and drought-ravaged Great Plains in the 1930s, intent on battling the dust and healing the land. As a college-educated geologist working for the U.S. government, Rosa Jean "RJ" Evans must find her place in a small farming town that welcomes neither a woman in authority nor changes to their way of life.

Inspired by actual events during the Great Depression and Dust Bowl environmental disaster, *Peculiar Savage Beauty* is a parable about man's quest to dominate the land and nature's refusal to be conquered. Beating back the dust is a daily battle for the people living in the devastated Great Plains. It's a clash that creates unlikely alliances. As RJ learns she must rely on her adversaries if she is to survive the dangers of the Dust Bowl, she also grows to realize that she – like the land itself – is in desperate need of healing.

My Dust Bowl research began many years ago with a documentary titled "Black Blizzard." I had been clicking through the television channels, when it popped up on the screen. It was gripping. The idea of living through such brutal dust storms intrigued me.

Motivated by the vague potential of writing a novel based on such an experience, I eventually watched more documentaries, read numerous books, and studied hundreds of historic photos. Images of rolling sand dunes and layers of dust were etched in my mind. They were terrifying and, oddly, beautiful.

All my research led me to formulate a story about environmental disaster and hard economic times. A theme began to develop around human nature and overcoming personal tragedy. At the heart of it all would be a strong female protagonist – a young woman with a great deal she could teach, as well as a great deal to learn.

Many months later, a video by sand artist Ilana Yahav appeared in my social media feed (most likely because of my countless Google searches containing the words *dust* and *sand*). Yahav told the story of "One Man's Dream" through performance art with evolving scenes created in sand on a light table.[7] I was mesmerized. After watching several more of Yahav's videos, I knew my novel-in-progress would involve some sort of sand art. How, exactly, that would take shape still was not clear to me.

The final *aha* moment happened when my son came home from school with an etching he had made on black paper. His high school art teacher had introduced us both to something new. Scratchboard paper. With this art medium, the artist scratches off the dark top coat of the paper to reveal a white layer beneath. In a form of engraving, the artist creates an image by adding in the highlights rather than the image itself. Once again, the Internet provided me with a visual – a tutorial of this new-to-me art form. And just like that, I could picture one of my novel characters etching beautiful images on ugly, dust-covered windows.

In the novel's earliest iterations, it had no elements of art. I struggled to formulate a way to incorporate it. Woody also did not yet exist. He made his first appearance as a minor character about halfway through the first draft. He was originally intended to simply be one of several quirky town's people my main character, RJ, would encounter. Almost without my knowing it, Woody began hanging out in more and more scenes. He was a compelling character, I finally realized, someone who deserved more attention. It sounds flakey, I know. But this is sometimes how a story takes shape when a writer gives in fully to the process.

A rough outline and more than half the novel already had been written. It was hard to abandon all that. Still, I started anew, without an outline, on a novel featuring Woody as a main character – as a brilliant though misunderstood young man, as an artist of sorts. The novel then had three main characters. The evolution of their friendships became the crux of the story. It was at that point that events and scenes began to really flow from my mind to the page. It was at that point I knew the pain of starting over again had been worth it.

Sometime during final copyedits, I stumbled upon a "Dirty Car Guy" article online. (Thanks once again to the mixed blessing of search engines, cookies, and target marketing.) Scott Wade travels the world etching remarkably detailed pictures on dirty cars and windows. I was dumbstruck at how close his artwork came to what I had been picturing in my mind's eye for years.

The final draft of *Peculiar Savage Beauty* is far different than the story I had initially set out to write. Thank goodness for that. In my experience, the key to success as a novelist is not so much in finding the right ideas, but in allowing time for the right ideas to find you.

Telling the Story

> "Forget about becoming a great writer. Work instead on writing great stories."
> – William Tapply, American mystery writer

Author Anne Perry once asked, "Is there any age or society that doesn't respond to 'Tell me a story'?" The answer, of course, is no. We all love a good story, and it's not just for entertainment. It's for survival.

Stories are how we learn from other's mistakes; how we know that petting that lion on the Serengeti might not be the smartest idea and how we know that looking both ways before crossing the street will help keep us from getting run over.

In her book *Wired for Story*, author Lisa Cron talks about what makes a story a story. She uses insights from neuroscience to guide the writer, the storyteller. [8]

"We think in story. It's hardwired in our brain. It's how we make strategic sense of the otherwise overwhelming world around us," she writes.

"Simply put, the brain constantly seeks meaning from all the input thrown at it, yanks out what's important for our survival on a need-to-know basis, and tells a story about it, based on what it knows of our past experience with it, how we feel about it, and how it might affect us."

Cron asserts that a story is just not about something that happens or even what the main character does when something happens. Story is about how the main character changes as a result of what happens. "Stories are about how we, rather than the world around us, change."

Her book is full of good stuff, broken down with "cognitive secrets" and "story secrets," as well as writing myths and realities. One chapter in particular explores the importance of zeroing in on your point when writing. She presents the ideas this way:

Cognitive secret

When the brain focuses its full attention on something, it filters out all unnecessary information.

Story secret

To hold the brain's attention, everything in a story must be there on a need-to-know basis.

Thus, every detail, every character, every scene, and every action should move the reader closer to the point of your story. If it doesn't move the reader closer to your point, then it shouldn't be there. It's the difference between simply telling the reader about "stuff that happens" to your characters and showing

the reader how your characters changed, for better or
for worse.

As you write and edit, be on the lookout for
historical facts and descriptive passages that, while
they may be fascinating or lovely, do not move the
story forward. Such prose needs to go. It can be
painful to cut words lovingly and expertly drawn, but
it is necessary to holding your reader's attention.

This doesn't mean there is no room for historical
and descriptive detail. It only means you must put
such detail to the "story test."

In *The Snow Child*, author Eowyn Ivey includes
many descriptive passages about the rugged and
beautiful Alaskan frontier landscape. At first blush, it
may seem indulgent or unnecessary to the story. Yet,
as the story progresses, the reader learns how the
theme of man's relationship with nature (both his
desire and his inability to control it, for one) is critical
to the growth and development of several characters.
Thus, descriptive language and historical detail that
puts the reader in the Alaskan wilderness in the early

1900s is critical and passes the story test with high marks.

The same applies to unique bits of information we uncover during the course of our research. What if a famous historical figure lived in the same city and time in which your novel is set? Would including that celebrity in your novel be merely name-dropping? Or would it add dimension and perspective to the protagonist's journey? It depends. The question to ask yourself is, again, does including him or her move the story forward?

A few of the advance readers for my historical novel *All Different Kinds of Free* suggested I remove the scenes and references to Charles Dickens from my book. They said it felt like name-dropping (these were all folks in the publishing business in one form or another). Other advance readers loved the Dickens sections and encouraged me to leave them in (interestingly, these folks were mostly readers and fellow writers).

What to do? To help me decide, I did a quick review of the first historical novel I ever read (and loved), *Ragtime* by E.L. Doctorow. I was in high school when I first read it, and at that time I hated "history."

Here's the back-cover blurb from my now dog-eared paperback copy:

> "*Ragtime* is set in America at the beginning of the century. Its characters: three remarkable families whose lives become entwined with people whose names are Henry Ford, Emma Goldman, Harry Houdini, J.P. Morgan, Evelyn Nesbit, Sigmund Freud, Emiliano Zapata."[9]

That description sounded suspiciously like "history" to me, not a juicy novel. Boy, was I wrong. Murder, magic, sex, money, racial tension, intrigue, love, betrayal: this book had it all. I especially loved that it included well-known historical figures along with the stories of average people. It was my first lesson, really, in how history is a part of our everyday lives.

This sort of name-dropping isn't limited to celebrities, either, or to historical fiction. Writers of contemporary fiction often include references to celebrities, name brands, pop culture, and current events. Such references, as long as they don't distract from the story, help put the fictional characters' lives and stories in context for the reader. They add dimension.

My first novel was inspired by the little-known U.S. Supreme Court case Prigg v. Pennsylvania and Margaret Morgan, the alleged run-away slave at the heart of the case. I hadn't specifically set out to include famous people in my fictional rendering of Margaret's story.

During my research, however, I stumbled upon the fact that Charles Dickens had vacationed in the United States and visited Washington, D.C. the same year the pivotal court case took place, 1842. Then I learned Dickens wrote a book about his trip. I read

American Notes as part of my research, and Dickens' thoughts and impressions on slavery ended up being an important plot point in my novel. It influenced a key character's growth. It had to stay.

My research also had uncovered that Edgar Allan Poe lived in Philadelphia (one of the main settings of my novel) during the same time my main character lived there. In fact, he later said the race riots he had witnessed in Philadelphia during that time inspired some of his future macabre works. How cool was that?

I worked long and hard to somehow weave in that juicy historical tidbit. In the end, it just didn't fit. It was intriguing, but it didn't add to value to Margaret's story. It didn't move *her* story forward. It had to go.

> "In today's marketplace successful nonfiction has to be unbelievable, while successful fiction must be believable."
> – Jerry Jenkins, American novelist and biographer

It's hard to know when to stick to historical record/facts and when to take creative liberties when writing fiction about real-life people or events. Though every novel is different, the story test still applies.

I have edited and critiqued hundreds of novels and manuscripts. Many times, my feedback highlighted a certain scene, character action, or event that felt unrealistic or couldn't possibly have happen the way it was written. Almost always, the writer's response was, "But it *did* happen that way." Perhaps it did. But that doesn't that doesn't matter if it can't pass the story test.

A fiction writer's allegiance is to the story. Historical accuracy is wonderful and important to fiction, but only if it adds to the story being told. If it detracts from the story, then it's detriment.

Ask the following question as you write and edit: Does this historical fact move the story forward? No? Then get out that red pen, cut the section out, and make up something that *does* move the story forward.

In *All Different Kinds of Free*, one of the supporting characters was based on a successful black entrepreneur living in Philadelphia at the same time Margaret did. Both were real people. Did they ever meet in real life? Probably not. But by weaving their stories together, I produced more intensity in Margaret's story. I implied that the tragedy she experienced had reach beyond just her life and her family's. (I happen to believe that's true, by the way, even though I don't have any hard evidence to back it up.) So, while that part of my novel isn't 100 percent historically accurate, it advances the story in a way that is more compelling than the strict facts could have.

> "I don't think writers should write about answers. I think writers should write about questions."
> – Paul Haggis, Canadian screenwriter

Speaking as a reader, there are few things more annoying than a novelist who believes she has all the answers. Everyone reads fiction for different reasons, but ultimately we all hope to be entertained rather than lectured. That's not to say entertaining fiction can only be happy and inconsequential.

Both of my novels address weighty events in U.S. history – slavery and environmental ruin, discrimination and economic disaster. When weaving a tale with subject matter like that, an author walks a fine line between shedding light on something heavy and beating her readers over the head with it. As a former journalist, I suppose I will always strive to enlighten readers with my research and writing. But I never, ever want to lecture them.

All that being said, it is infinitely more practical and less grueling to write a lecture.

How do you write with enlightenment and empathy about someone whose beliefs you despise? How do you present two sides of a story that, in hindsight, seems painfully one-sided? And how do you include key historical facts in your prose without it reading like a textbook?

The secret to mastering such feats can be summed up in two pieces of oft-repeated (and pretty annoying) writing advice; one, "show, don't tell," and two, "write about people, not characters." It's not as simple as it sounds (which is what makes it so annoying). But a writer who practices and refines those techniques can reveal even the darkest elements of the human psyche and still leave her readers feeling uplifted and hopeful when they turn the last page.

Examples of this mastery can be found between the covers of the following novels (aka, writing manuals): *The Light Between Oceans* by M.L. Stedman, *Pictures of You* by Caroline Leavitt, *The Railway Man's Wife* by Ashley Hay, *The Women in the Castle* by Jessica Shattuck and *The Orchardist* by Amanda Coplin.

If you want to understand how to write in multiple perspectives about gut-wrenching, heart-breaking events with beauty and hope, study these books.

In the meantime, here's an example from my novel, *Peculiar Savage Beauty*, that illustrates these writing techniques (though I'll make no claims as to whether I've yet succeeded in mastering my own advice).

While RJ is the main character of the novel, the story has several other key protagonists and multiple antagonists. Sometimes the reader may have a hard time distinguishing which is which. That would make me do a jazz-hands happy-dance, because I didn't want to write a story populated with clear-cut good guys and bad guys. I wanted to take readers inside the heads of average people – people like you and like me – and have them become friends. I wanted readers to alternately cheer at these new friends' triumphs and virtues, and shake fists at their blunders and shortcomings.

During a scene with RJ and Harvey, a young unmarried farmer, I weave in a little farming history and also reveal some of the characters' personality traits.

RJ is frustrated and angry that the locals wouldn't give her a chance to explain new conservation techniques at the farmers' union meeting. Over late-night pie and coffee in a small diner, she laments this to Harvey, saying the men don't respect her or her expertise.

Harvey allows her to complain, then points out that she didn't give the farmers a chance to express their ideas either and that she assumed she knows more than they do. His approach is gentle, yet firm, almost paternal, which gives the reader insight to how Harvey views the world and RJ in particular.

She realizes Harvey is correct, and RJ suddenly feels embarrassed and ashamed of her actions. But I didn't write, "She was ashamed and embarrassed." Instead, I showed that emotion to the reader through RJ's physical response. She casts her eyes down. She opens her mouth as if to speak, then stops. She pushes her food around the plate with a fork, as the light bulb buzzes above their heads and the quietness of the moment becomes uncomfortable.

Through casual conversation over pie and coffee, several important objectives are met – the novel's plot is advanced, the relationship between RJ and Harvey progresses to a new level, and some historical context on how the Dust Bowl disaster evolved is presented. Most importantly, the reader enjoys the exchange between the RJ and Harvey, wonders what will happen next, and turns the page.

Forging a Path

> "Writing a story is like crossing a stream, now I'm on this rock, now I'm on this rock, now I'm on this rock."
> – Ann Beattie, American novelist

When the time comes to assemble your ideas and begin writing, is it better to work from an outline or write by the seat of your pants? This question has been the subject of debate among writers for ions.

With an outline, you have a map. With the seat-of-you-pants approach, you simply write and see where the story takes you.

The common criticism with outlines is that it is too restrictive and can prevent you from exploring new ideas and plot twists as they come to you. The common criticism of the "pantser" approach is that unplanned writing typically leads to major revisions. (Cold hard truth alert: no matter what approach you take, you had better plan on major revisions and rewrites. There's no good writing, only good rewriting. It's a worn-out axiom, because it's true.)

There is no correct answer to the outline or seat-of-your-pants question. Just try one. If it works, great! If not, try the other. If that works, great! If not, combine the two and see how that works. Keep in mind, too, that one method may work well for you as you draft your first book and then fail you as you work on your next. Writing is hard. In the words of Tom Hanks, starring as a baseball coach in the movie *A League of Their Own*, "It's supposed to be hard. The hard is what makes it great. If it was easy, everyone would do it."

A hybrid of the two approaches works best for me.

I begin with a rough outline that includes key events, plot points, and scenes – all pretty much in chronological order. As I write, the outline changes and evolves. Some events are replaced by others, or new scenes and characters are added. Every so often, I update the outline to reflect what I've written so far. In many respects, I write by the seat of my pants and see where it takes me. When I get lost or hit a brick wall, I go back to my map – my outline – and get my bearings again. I use a map, but I don't lock myself into one particular route to get me where I want to go.

The key to my hybrid approach is that I know essentially where I want to end up; I know the overall idea of the story, the big picture.

Putting It Together

Before people had tablets and smartphones, we occupied time with jigsaw puzzles. I still enjoy them. My mom taught me to put together all the edge pieces first, to create the outline, and then fill in the middle.

In school, that seemed to be the conventional wisdom from my writing teachers, too. Start with an outline, and fill in the details. For better or for worse, I've never been very good at following conventional wisdom.

When doing jigsaws, I would try to work the edges first. I really would. But then, what's this here? Could it be part of an elbow? Maybe it's an ear. And what about this piece? It has the same peachy hue, maybe it goes with this one. Ah ha! Little by little, section by scattered section, the big picture would eventually come together. Inevitably, the final piece to snap into place would be some flat-edged rascal that seemed to be lost until the very end.

My writing generally takes shape the same way. Even for the shortest magazine article, I struggle with sticking to an outline. A quote jumps out at me. An anecdote begs to be fleshed out. A statistic yearns to be researched. Then all the pieces get shifted and rearranged again and again, until the big picture finally materializes. The opening paragraphs are usually the last thing I write.

Multiply that by about a hundred, and you have a pretty good idea of how I write novels – little by little, scene by scattered scene, until the last plot point finally snaps into place.

All Different Kinds of Free was inspired by actual events. It tells the story of Margaret Morgan, a free woman of color in 1830s America whose perfect life was shattered when she was kidnapped and forced into slavery. It took me more than five years to figure out all the plot points, to write and assemble all the scenes and chapters of the book. The first scene I wrote, the one I thought would be the opening scene, ended up somewhere in the middle.

For a long time, the knowledge that this is my writing process was daunting as hell. Oh, it's fine for a fifteen-hundred-word article that takes a few weeks to complete. But apply it to novel writing, and you're looking at years of writing and re-arranging for every book. Finally, I came to accept that writing a novel (and doing it well) simply takes as long as it takes.

Freelance writer and memoir author Jessica Handler also thinks it's OK to write out of order. In fact, she encourages it.

"Just because your story follows a timeline doesn't mean you have to write it linearly," she wrote in an article for *The Writer* (May 2011). "If you're inspired to write a scene other than the one that comes next in your manuscript, go for it. You can put the story in the right order later."

Handler's advice is comforting as I hammer away at my third novel. My outline is sketchy, at best. I have several dozen scenes and vignettes written; they feel a bit random and unrelated right now. That's OK. I know the big picture is there somewhere, waiting to reveal itself. As I shift and re-arrange all the sections, I know that final flat-edged piece is just waiting to be snapped into place.

Taking Handler's insight a step further, just because your story follows a timeline doesn't mean you have to *present* it linearly either. For example, one memorable *Seinfeld* sitcom episode aired backwards, scene by scene. It featured the gang flying to India for the wedding of a woman who had long been one of Elaine's archenemies. Why on Earth would they spend the time and money on such a trip? Because the scenes played out in reverse, we didn't get the answer to that question until the end of the show.

Would that particular episode have been as funny or interesting had we learned the reason in the opening scene? Probably not.

When I was working on the early drafts of my first novel, the opening five or so chapters in particular felt like one of those Jumble word puzzles – in which the letters are all mixed up and you have a clue to solve or question to answer. I had to re-arrange those chapters several times before the order finally felt right, before the answer became clear.

Does your writing sometimes feel backwards? Don't give up on it. Just keep writing and keep moving pieces of the story around. Run it backwards and forwards. When it's right, you'll know it (even if that means the story plays out backwards), and you'll hold your readers to the very end... or the beginning.

"It's never too late – in fiction or in life – to revise."
– Nancy Thayer, American novelist

The first book I wrote was a murder mystery. The Missing Clock features murder, suspense, a smooth-talking private eye and a surprise plot-twist at the end, Scooby Doo-style. I was eight when I wrote it. The book was neatly bound with two staples. It also included a color illustration of the clock in question, a priceless heirloom encased in gold and sparkling gems.

My mom, a voracious reader, was my first fan and my first critic.

"I like it," she said. "But you should describe the clock instead of just drawing a picture."

It was my first lesson in the importance of revision, though I didn't know it at the time. My second lesson came years later from my high school English teacher, Mr. Churbuck, senior year. Revision, he said, was vital because it gives you a chance to add what's missing. And there's always something missing. The only way to earn an A in his class was to turn in a minimum of three drafts with every assignment – one handwritten, complete with scratch marks, scribbles and arrows; one typed and littered with red-inked edits; and a typed final draft, which he would inevitably litter with red-inked edits of his own. By the end of the year, I was turning in four or five drafts, stacks of edits so thick they were barely harnessed by my second-hand stapler, and reveling in the fact that the only red mark on the final draft from Mr. C was an A+.

My mom's fierce love of books likely fueled my early desire to write; and Mr. Churbuck's fierce devotion to the art and craft of revision is what made me a writer.

Because of Mr. Churbuck's influence, my processes for writing and revision are inextricably intertwined. He taught his students to write fat first drafts, to include everything we believed to be relevant. Once that task was complete, it was time to take out the red pen and start cutting. Delete redundant thoughts. Erase overused clichés. Tighten run-on sentences. Remove irrelevant details. Then take that lean new draft and add more meat, add what is missing.

In short, he taught us to be both prolific writers and capable editors.

After practicing and applying this technique for decades, I learned how to write lean and clean first drafts. This saves time on editing, thus providing more opportunity to add the meat. When working with a manuscript in the neighborhood of one-hundred-thousand-words, you need all the time and opportunity you can get.

Editing the Beast

Once I have a complete draft (which is usually pretty awful), I embark upon multiple editing phases. Each phase has an important role in strengthening and polishing the text. These steps are the writer's job, long before an official editor ever lays eyes on the manuscript. It's hard, necessary work. It can mean the difference between being offered a publishing contract and being relegated to the slush pile for eternity.

The following sections detail my process – and thus, recommendations – for editing a manuscript. First, a few tips before you begin:

1. **Accept that editing takes a lot of time.** You'll likely read through and edit the full manuscript three-to-five times, perhaps more. You may also reread and edit particular sections dozens of times. Be comforted in knowing the work will get better with each pass.

2. **Save and rename your draft document before you begin each round of edits.** This collection of drafts will be helpful as you cut, revise, move and add prose. There may be times you'll want to back-peddle on something you've changed; having the previous draft intact will be a godsend.

3. **Keep separate, corresponding files for notes during every phase of your editing.** This can be an electronic files or spreadsheets, via writing software such as Scrivener, or something more old school like handwritten notes in a spiral notebook or on three-by-five index cards. Do what feels most comfortable (or, at any rate, is the least painful). Whatever method you choose, be meticulous in your note-taking. Make sure notes contain details like chapters, page numbers, and character names, as well as keywords for themes, plot twists and subplots. This will make chapters, scenes and sentences easier to find and move around when the time comes.

Big Picture

Key plot points, characterization, overall story arc: these are big picture elements.

On the first read through, look for holes in the plot and subplots. Has the main character(s) done enough things and made enough decisions to complete the personal transformation from Point A to Point B? Did all the things happen in the middle of the story that need to happen to make sure that Point B makes sense in the end?

Does the book have a beginning, middle, and end? You might be surprised how often writers have those three elements so firmly in their minds that they don't realize all three haven't actually made it to the page.

On the next read-through, pay close attention to each of the secondary and supporting characters. Maintain a list or spreadsheet that documents pages and scenes in which each character appears. This provides another perspective on the big picture. Are there too many characters? If one appears in only a scene or two, perhaps that character should be cut

and a more important character with too-few scenes
can be inserted there.

It's important to think of all the characters as
multi-dimensional people. Do they have enough
personality and back story of their own to resonate
with the reader? If not, such characters will feel flat
and contrived, mere props inserted to move the story
along as things happen to the main character.
Supporting characters don't need a huge amount of
detail; they just need enough to give readers the sense
that everyone has a life of his or her own, has a story
to be told, even if it's not in this book.

Make another pass through the manuscript from
beginning to end in which you focus on the emotional
level of the work. Nineteenth-century British novelist
and dramatist Charles Reade famously advised, "Make
'em laugh; make 'em cry; make 'em wait." This is the
time to ensure your story does all of these.

Does page one have a strong hook? Is there plenty
of suspense throughout the book to keep the reader
turning pages? Make sure every chapter ends with a

cliffhanger or unanswered question so the reader must know what will happen next. Does the conclusion provide enough satisfaction that the reader won't feel cheated, yet enough pull that he won't want the story to end?

This is also the opportunity to layer more emotion into pivotal scenes. Creating scenes with strong, authentic emotion – especial sensations like love, grief, betrayal, forgiveness – typically requires a writer to take multiple runs at them.

There is a slave auction scene in *All Different Kinds of Free* that I found terribly painful to write. It highlights the way in which families were separated and sold to multiple people or locations. Often those family members never saw one another again and were never given the chance to say good-bye. As a mother, I didn't want to even imagine the kind of pain that would cause. I procrastinated writing the scene literally for years.

When the time came when the auction scene had to be written to complete the novel, I blew through it

as fast as I could. That first draft was short and
lacking in emotion; but it was written. That gave me
words on the page, words I could go back to and
rework, which I probably did six or more times. Each
time I went back to it, I added a bit more action, a
whisper more sensory detail – all to help the reader
see and feel what the people at the auction were
seeing and feeling.

It's a bit like assembling a cake. You start with the
essentials – a cake base, a layer of frosting, another
layer of cake to top it off. Then you keep layering on,
building up. The more layers you add, the richer the
cake (or the scene) becomes. Just keep piling on until
the scene reaches the emotional height that it needs.

Fine-Tuning

**Once you've honed the plot, characters, and
emotions,** you can begin to drill down and fine-tune
other key elements. Be on the look-out for overused
words and phrases, awkward shifts in point of view,
and inconsistencies in tense. You also want to pay

attention to theme and symbolism – literary elements add depth to a story.

Theme is the main idea of the story; though a story can also contain additional underlying themes. (Think big ideas such as *good vs. evil, man vs. man, man vs. nature* or a combination of ideas.) Theme can also be less stringent, especially in more literary novels. It can be a question or an idea. For example, the primary theme of *All Different Kinds of Free* is slavery (man against man); an underlying theme is that freedom has many meanings. These ideas should flow organically through the story and be clear to the reader before reaching "The End."

"One problem with talking about theme is that any discussion necessarily makes 'theme' sound like something extra that is added to a story at the end, like cheese baked on top of a casserole," wrote Donald Maass in his book, *Writing the Breakout Novel.*[10] "If authentic, theme is not something apart from story but something intrinsic to it. It is not embedded, but rather emerges."

Symbolism is used to enhance and strengthen a
story's theme. A symbol is generally a physical object
(e.g., the ring in J.R.R. Tolkien's *Lord of the Rings*, the
dust in *Peculiar Savage Beauty*, or the newspapers in
News of the World). Though it also can be an animal,
phrase, or just about anything that packs a powerful
idea into a simple package (e.g. the prayer in *Ordinary
Grace*, the extended metaphor in *Animal Farm*, or the
color red in *The Scarlet Letter*).

As with theme, symbolism needs to be carefully
crafted and woven through the story, so that it
doesn't feel fabricated to the reader. Maas explains it
better than I.

"Evoking symbols is often a matter of making use
of what is already there," he wrote. "If a symbol
would otherwise naturally occur in a story, use it. It
will not feel stagy. In fact, many readers may not
consciously notice it."

Nitty-Gritty

This is the more tangible copyediting phase. It includes correcting things that spelling and grammar software miss: typographical errors, missing words, incorrect words, inconsistent facts. Many writers will perform this step by reading backwards; it's a trick to help spot glaring mistakes that are all-too-easy to miss after having read the manuscript multiple times.

Getting to "The End"

Another topic Holland Rogers addresses in *Word Work*[11] is goal setting. He does a nice job of defining what he calls performance goals, which come in two varieties – *certainty goals* and *expectation goals*. Certainty goals are ones you have complete control over, and as a result help reduce the anxiety you can feel when you begin to lose control of a project (or think you're losing control, even if you aren't).

He offers up the following example for a book project he had with a tight deadline:

"I set an expectation goal of a chapter a day. This is what I fully expected to be able to do, and it was what my calendar called for. But this goal alone would have made me anxious at the start of every day, so it was supported (or ameliorated) by a certainty goal: Every day, I would write on the current chapter for six hours.

I couldn't always produce a chapter every day. Some days I got hung up on some plot difficulty or another. (Thankfully, there were some days when I wrote a chapter and a half.) But every single day, I could guarantee that I'd be at my desk for those six hours."

When applying this concept of expectation and certainty to your own writing, consider what is reasonable for you given your own abilities and time constraints.

Some writers commit to at least an hour of writing per day, which most people can fit into their day even if they work a full-time job and/or have to take care of a family. Set the alarm clock for an hour earlier. Write for an hour after you put the kids (or spouse) to bed. Write during your lunch break. Log out of social media for an hour a day, and write instead.

Other writers need bigger chunks of time to be productive and keep a project moving forward. This is the category into which I fall. Because I have a flexible work schedule, I can block chunks of time for my novel writing into my work week. For example, when I became serious about completing my first novel (which I had chipped away at for several years), I began blocking off Fridays for novel writing. No other work on Fridays. No client calls. No kiddo dentist appointments. Just eight hours of novel work. Sometimes that also meant working at night the other days of the week to meet client deadlines. It was worth the sacrifice. Within six months, I had finally completed a solid first draft.

One author I know finds success by committing to write a certain amount per day – say one-thousand words – no matter how long it takes. If she finishes in only three hours, she stops writing and shifts to research or marketing for the remainder of her day. If those thousand words take ten hours, she keeps her butt in the seat until she hits her goal. Other authors will set a word-count goal for the week, which offers a bit more day-to-day flexibility.

Once you decide on a structure for your goals, you must carve out time from your life to work toward them. Time won't just fall in your lap. You'll have to give up something else. Maybe that means three hours after dinner a few times a week, while the loved ones watch TV or play a board game (think of it like taking a night-school class). Or working for six hours every other Saturday, while family and friends are out having fun at the park, the movies or the nightclub.

It takes sacrifice to reach an ambitious goal. In my case, blocking Fridays for non-paying novel work also meant taking on more corporate freelance writing projects and fewer magazine articles. Corporate writing pays more than magazine writing; it can also be a lot less fun. I gave up the fun magazine work to earn more money in fewer hours, to make time for novel writing.

Despite all the talk about goals, achieving success in writing (in anything, frankly) is more about developing a sustainable process. For me, devoting Fridays to my novel only worked because I had created a sustainable process for working fewer hours while still paying my bills.

Another good thing about focusing on process is that it can be elastic. The problem with goals is that they imply a rigid either-or conflict.

"Either you achieve your goal and are successful or you fail and you are a disappointment. You mentally box yourself into a narrow version of happiness," wrote James Clear, author of Atomic Habits. "This is misguided. It is unlikely that your actual path through life will match the exact journey you had in mind when you set out. It makes no sense to restrict your satisfaction to one scenario when there are many paths to success." [12]

When my writing goals are too precise, I rarely meet them because my method of writing is anything but precise. Many of my writing days take me one step forward and two steps back. For example, I might draft a new five-hundred-word scene, and then cut a thousand words from a different section. Did I add to my total word count? No. Can I consider that progress on my novel? You bet.

"New goals don't deliver new results. New lifestyles do. And a lifestyle is not an outcome, it is a process," Clear wrote. "For this reason, all of your energy should go into building better habits, not chasing better results."

Set some goals. Experiment with different ways to meet them. Change course when needed, until you find a process that works for you.

Balancing Research

> "All good books are alike in that they are
> truer than if they had really happened."
> – Ernest Hemingway,
> American journalist and novelist

**For readers to embrace the inherent truth in
fiction,** the work must feel authentic. It's why writers
are always in search of infinitesimal crumbs of truth
to weave into their fictional prose. It's why research
and nonfiction reading is a vital part of every fiction
writer's job.

Science fiction writers must know enough about
actual science to make whatever mind-boggling
concepts they have imagined seem plausible. Fantasy
writers must draw on real-life elements that will help

readers suspend their disbelief of the fantastical. Even writers of contemporary fiction must mind true-to-life details, because a careless error can sometimes derail a reader's satisfaction with the entire story.

Historical fiction writers bear perhaps the heaviest research burden. Readers of such novels are sticklers for accuracy. Make one tiny reference to a brassier in a story set in the 1800s, and you will feel the full force of the anachronism hammer rain upon you (I speak from experience).

All this means that serious writers read a lot, so much more than we can ever use in our writing. We sometimes will read an entire nonfiction book in search of one small tidbit of information to bring more truth to our work.

Jay Boyer's play "Poaching Deer in Northern Arizona" is a case-in-point. Boyer is an accomplished film scholar, poet and playwright. His work has been produced and read in venues across the United States and around the world, including New York, Los

Angeles, and London. One thing Boyer has not done is hunt deer.

So he set out to learn as much as he could about deer hunting to add authenticity to his story. He studied how to hand-load gunpowder into shotgun shell casings. He learned the proper way to field dress a deer so that the meat does not spoil. He wrote copious notes on the subject. In the end, though, the vast majority of Boyer's research sat on the shelf.

"I did a great deal of research, and I used just a brush stroke or two in the play," Boyer said. "I wound up using a little bit about shell casings, and I wound up using a little bit about how you prepare a deer. But I was only comfortable doing that once I had learned probably enough about it to write a long and extensive article on each issue."

That process of researching, drafting, and throwing away is more the rule than the exception when it comes to effective writing, regardless of the length or genre of the piece. In researching my second novel, I read no fewer than twenty-five nonfiction books and countless articles about the Great Depression, the Dust Bowl, farming, geology, auto mechanics, ecology, land surveying, food canning, quilting, the Civilian Conservation Corps, the New Deal, and so much more. I assembled binders full of notes. I abandoned a lot of it when it was time to write.

Again, people who read fiction are in it for the story, not a history lesson. They want to be immersed in the time and place. They want to become invested in the fates of the characters.

"Historical fiction makes us feel," said Susan Vreeland, a bestselling historical novelist. "It presents to us a truth more human than what history books present."

So, while fiction writers strive for accuracy, all that research is not solely about getting all the facts straight. It's also about getting to know our characters and understanding their stories. And, for that reason, most writers love doing it.

"Approaching research from a place of curiosity and wonder shapes the author's relationship with that information," Dana Chamblee Carpenter wrote in a column for *Writer's Digest*.[13] She's the author of *The Bohemian Trilogy*, a series of historical paranormal novels. "What we learn comes to us as a living thing, like magic, and we handle it with care, folding it into the story like one might tenderly fold egg whites into a batter. This way, the rich details lift the story up rather than weigh it down."

Complicating the writer's job even further is the reality that every person's "truth" is different. Our unique life experiences shape our perceptions of the world around us. Early in my writing career, my journalism training rendered my opinions regarding fact and fiction pretty much in black and white. As I got a bit more life experience under my belt (venturing into public relations, communications, marketing, and finally, fiction writing), I began to understand just how fuzzy the line between fact and fiction truly is in all writing.

Still, exposing that intrinsic truth of which
Hemingway spoke should always be the writer's goal,
even when she knows that absolutes are impossible.
Natalia Sylvester ruminated on this idea as she was
fine-tuning her debut novel, *Chasing the Sun.*

"The best we might ever hope for is to write what
is 'truest' or 'true at the moment,' because this, too,
can always change," she said. "How an author
chooses to tell a story – by sticking to what we know,
by venturing into what one can imagine – is as much
about the writer as it is about the story."

> "Life is like riding a bicycle. To keep your
> balance, you must keep moving."
> – Albert Einstein,
> German-born theoretical physicist

Einstein's analogy applies to writing, too. As
someone who loves doing research and finding
obscure historical tidbits, I could research forever.

And it's so darn easy now that you can go online and find anything you could possibly want to know. As great as that is, it can also be a hindrance to finishing a manuscript. Writing is harder, as much as I love it, and I'm often all-too-willing to procrastinate it. When I have a tough scene to write, for example, I tell myself I need to do just a bit more research first. Yet, to keep my balance, I must keep moving, keep writing.

There's a quote by the late author Tom Clancy that I keep close at hand to help me stay on track. "You must write the book, else there is no book." Simple, yet wise. You may have gathered a great deal of research already, or you still may be working to find the historical insights you seek. Either way, keep in mind the purpose is to write.

Following is an abbreviated look at the approach I take to balance research and writing. While my focus is on writing historical novels, the strategy can work effectively for any long-form genre.

1. **Big picture research.** For this, I read books and
   watch documentaries that offer an overview of
   the time and place in history where my story
   unfolds. I want to gain a general understanding of
   the key historical figures and events. This gets my
   creative juices flowing. It also helps me to begin
   drafting a rough outline of my novel – how are
   the story, themes, and plot points influenced by
   the historical time, place, and events? The big
   picture research puts the story in context.

2. **Character research.** Here's when I begin drilling
   down to the day-to-day lives of average people
   living in my chosen time and location. Where did
   they work, shop, or go to school? What did they
   eat, wear, and do for fun? How did they get where
   they needed to go? Getting a handle on daily life
   helps me to draft brief profiles of my key
   characters and ensure the characters are
   multidimensional. These details will also add
   authenticity to the story and help create a strong
   sense of time and place for the reader.

3. **Writing.** Once I have a sense of the story, plot and subplots, and the characters' lives, personalities, and motivations, I begin writing. As I write, I make note of areas in which I need to do additional research. In my overall plan for novel completion, I designate specific time each week for writing and specific time for doing more research. That way, I'm less tempted to stop writing when the writing gets tough and instead go in search of a new historical fact or tidbit. I tell myself, "I will look that up tomorrow. Keep writing today."

4. **Revising and weaving.** Once I have a rough draft, I go back and start filling in the holes. Sometimes that means adding more historical perspective to create a strong time and place (which may mean new/additional research in a specific area). Other times it may mean filling out characters that seem flat, adding more tension to dull scenes, or adding new scenes or chapters to better tell the story.

Hitting the Road

> "A desk is a dangerous place from which to
> view the world."
> – John Le Carré, British author

In her book *How to Write and Sell Historical Fiction*, author Persia Wooley includes two lengthy chapters on research trips.[14] Such trips can be little or big – a day trip to a local museum or a road trip to the Rocky Mountains. It really depends on who you are and what you are seeking.

"Only the writer can decide whether such a trip is worthwhile," she wrote.

"Some simply have no interest in going to their locations whereas others are willing to travel on the barest of shoestrings, without even a contract in their pockets, just to make certain they 'get it right' in their books."

I'm a fan of field trips.

Getting away from the desk and the computer can work wonders for your productivity; and the experiences you have can add dimension, authenticity, and life to your writing.

Museums, historic sites, cultural festivals, and re-enactments are a few examples. It's about conducting research, and it's about feeding creativity.

Feeding Creativity

> "Most of us harbor a secret belief that work has to be work and not play... This is not true."
> – Julia Cameron, *The Artist's Way*

Sometimes writing inspiration strikes in the oddest places. Years ago, I attended a Barrett-Jackson car auction event with my husband and son. I'm not into cars, but the boys were going and I wanted to spend the Sunday afternoon with them. The loose itinerary was to walk around looking at cars that would go on auction later in the week, eat some greasy food, and then head home in time to catch the fourth quarter of the Giants/Packers game.

Other than a stomach ache, I had no idea what to expect. I don't really give a rat's behind about horse power, reinforced chassis, or original miles. I'm nerdy. I like books and history, and books about history. So I was pleasantly surprised to discover the car show was oozing with history.

I was dazzled by a 1947 Bentley, which had won more than fifty "best of show" honors in car events through the years (and sold for a cool $2.75 million that week). Then there was the 1948 Tucker Torpedo, one of only fifty-one sedans produced in Chicago that year by American automobile designer and entrepreneur Preston Tucker (it sold for an astounding $2.9 million).

The 1964 Cadillac hearse that had carried President John F. Kennedy's body from Parkland Memorial Hospital to the airport at Love Field mesmerized me. As I watched the crowd quietly mill around the vehicle reading the signage explaining its historical significance, my mind raced with questions about the lives this vehicle had touched and where it had been the past fifty years.

Suddenly, I was swept up in a wave of ideas – historical and fictional characters appearing in my mind's eye, story plots taking shape in my day dreams as we walked the aisles of million-dollar cars. Then I saw a 1931 Ford model AA flatbed truck, and I was transported to another time and place altogether.

The novel I was drafting at the time was set in the 1930s American Dust Bowl, and my main character owned that very truck. The vehicle wasn't a critical element to the story – just a small historical detail to add authenticity to the work. My research online had uncovered vintage photographs of the Model AA, information about how and when it was made, and what it cost to buy new and used. None of that compared to standing next to the real deal.

I was surprised how small it was, so much shorter and lower to the ground than modern pick-up trucks. It made me wonder how the truck would handle on the rutted hardscrabble roads of the Depression-era Midwest. As I stood next to the vehicle (and fought the urge to ignore the "please do not touch" sign and run my hand along the cool, smooth hood), a scene formed in my mind like a black-and-white John Ford movie. I could see my novel's heroine climbing in, firing it up, and taking off down some dust-blown road.

Prior to that weekend, I had been struggling with my novel-in-progress, had hit a bit of a creative dry spell. That Sunday, I could have taken the opportunity to write in a quiet house while the boys were out, to muscle through my writer's block. The much touted butt-in-seat approach. Instead, I played hooky, at a car show of all places, and found the inspiration I needed to get my creative engine running again.

Connecting with Nature

> "Those who dwell among the beauties and mysteries of the earth are never alone or weary of life."
> – Rachel Carson,
> American conservationist and author

A curious epiphany followed the release of my second novel: yard work makes me a better writer. I've been blessed to receive many kind words about the writing, characters, and themes in *Peculiar Savage Beauty*, a historical novel set in the 1930s Dust Bowl. But one recent comment in particular made my heart soar and sparked that ah-ha moment. A reader, Lori Parker, wrote on Twitter, "Read this. You will love it. You will never forget it. And you will quite possibly go outside and plant something."

Nature and the outdoors have always been part of my life. I have vivid memories from childhood of playtime outside. There were forts and hideouts

among the bushes. There were rope swings on the
Mulberry tree. I ran a make-believe mud pie bakery in
my back yard. I led imaginary desert tours among the
prickly pear cacti and creosote bushes in my front
yard. As an adult, I hike in the desert near my home,
watch the birds feed and play outside my office
window, and sweat in the yard pulling weeds and
trimming plants.

The activity doesn't seem to matter. Stepping into
the sunshine and fresh air, slowing down to
appreciate the natural world, always has a positive
effect on my mood. As it turns out, that isn't the only
benefit. A body of research shows that connecting
with nature improves focus, creativity, and overall
health and quality of life.

A research team led by Masashi Soga conducted
meta-analysis of twenty-two recent case studies
examining the health benefits of gardening. The
studies reported a wide range of health outcomes,
including reductions in depression, anxiety and body
mass index, as well as increases in life satisfaction and

sense of community. Soga's project confirmed the
consistent findings across the range of ages, settings,
and other demographics explored in the studies.

"A regular dose of gardening can improve public
health," concluded Soga, in a 2017 *Preventive Medicine
Report* article.[15]

Child and nature advocate Richard Louv agrees. In
2005, he coined the term nature-deficit disorder in his
best-selling book, *Last Child in the Woods: Saving Our
Children from Nature-Deficit Disorder.*[16] According to the
author, his was the first book to bring together a
growing body of research indicating that direct
exposure to nature is essential for healthy childhood
development. It linked the lack of nature in the lives
of "today's wired generation" to an alarming rise in
childhood obesity, attention disorders, and
depression.

Louv's follow-up book in 2011 further explored
how the nature-deficit phenomenon impacts adults.
In *The Nature Principle: Reconnecting with Life in a Virtual
Age*[17], he raised the question, "What could our lives be

like if our days and nights were as immersed in nature as they are in technology?"

A 2014 study at the University of Sussex may have provided an answer. It discovered that constant media multitasking impacts the brain in negatives ways.[18] It compared magnetic resonance imaging (MRI) brain scans from two subsets of seventy-five individuals (gender, age, and education level did not differ significantly within the two subsets). Study participants who reported higher amounts of media multitasking were found to have smaller brain density in regions that regulate empathy and emotions, and control cognitive skills that enable organization, flexibility, and adaptability.

What's the bottom line of all this research?

Stepping away from technology and multitasking to connect with nature is good for both your body and your brain.

Thus, yard work makes me a better writer. It protects my brain from damage being done by a hectic life submerged in electronics and multitasking.

It sharpens my senses. It enables me to tune out the noise of daily life and focus more clearly on the stories I write.

The busyness of life doesn't allow me to go hiking, camping, or wildlife watching as often as I'd like. Still, I can always manage to fit in a short walk in the park or a few minutes in the yard to pull weeds. When all else fails, I take my work to a patio.

The perfume of fresh cut foliage. The sound of birds twittering, of lizards rustling in the underbrush. The burn of my muscles. The caress of the sun on my face, of a breeze in my hair. All this lifts my mood, boosts my brain and informs my writing. If it also encourages my readers to "go outside and plant something," all the better.

Confronting Fear

Writing is a lot like parenting. It's scary as hell, for one thing. You question yourself – your actions, your decisions – constantly. It's also hard to know when it's time to stop meddling with what you've created, when it's time to take a deep breath and let go.

It doesn't matter if the writing is a magazine article or a poem, a personal essay or a novel. It's hard to send it out into the big, bad world alone.

How do know if you've done all you can? How do you know if it's ready? The short answer is, you never know for sure until you do let go. That unknown can be intimidating, and it holds many people back. It locks them into the "I want to be a writer" mindset rather than letting them move into the "I am a writer" mindset. If you've provided your writing offspring with unconditional love, if you've given it all you have to give, then it's time to stare down the fear and let it go. Have faith. No one can soar without taking a leap.

All throughout my childhood, my parents had a mantra they'd say to me when I'd get worked up and worried about the future. "Nothing happens until it does." It's ironic, because they worried about things all the time and still do. It's sound wisdom, though, and I make a daily effort to embrace it. It's especially salient for fiction writers when it comes to the "life" portion of "the writing life."

As writers, we love to play the "what if?" game. We're relaxing at the coffee shop or waiting in line at the post office or pulling into the parking lot at the day job. Then it strikes. What if that guy who just bought a vanilla latte is secretly in love with the barista? What if the woman in line ahead of me is about to learn she has an incurable disease? What if the people sitting in that parked car are plotting to overthrow the government?

It's how compelling fiction is born.

Yet, we get so practiced at playing this game it often invades our writing pursuits in destructive ways. What if I spend years writing this novel and nobody reads it? What if I pour my heart into this book and then somebody else publishes one just like it before mine is complete? What if my writing sucks?

Sure, all those things could happen. Absolutely. Or not. Nothing happens until it does. Don't let the fear of failure paralyze you or even slow you down when it comes to chasing your dreams. Just write. Write the best damn novel or short story or magazine article or poem or (insert your dream here) that you can. Study the craft. Enjoy the process. And see what happens when it does.

Start asking yourself more positive questions. What if I spend years writing this novel and everybody loves it? What if I work hard on this novel and people say it's one of a kind? What if my writing shines?

One of my favorite quotes is from prolific writer and *New York Times* bestselling author Laurence Shames. He said, "Success and failure. We think of them as opposites, but they're really not. They're companions." He's spot on. Every day, I write something. Every day, I fail at it. And, every day, I improve as a writer. I see my shortcomings. I revise my prose. I succeed.

Here's a "what if" question for you, one you can print off and pin on your wall. "What if I work hard on this book and I learn something important about writing, about myself and about life?"

What if, indeed.

Embracing the Struggle

> "One day, in retrospect, the years of struggle
> will strike you as the most beautiful."
> – Sigmund Freud,
> Austrian neurologist and father of
> psychoanalysis

Writing a novel is a walk in the park, though not the leisurely walk you may be envisioning. It's like one particular, harrowing walk in the park I had with my dogs.

My rescue pup, a super-loveable German Sheppard mix, had some "issues" around other dogs when she was on leash. Maybe she was being protective of me. Maybe it was just a doggy dominance thing. The reason doesn't really matter. One day, during a hike in one of our many Phoenix desert preserves, we happened to cross paths with a rambunctious golden retriever and its owner. Both dogs pulled at their leashes, lunging toward one another with noisy growls and flying saliva. It was unclear if they wanted to play or fight, but we weren't about to risk finding out.

As I struggled to gain control of my unruly pup, I stumbled over a large rock in the trail and went sprawling into the dirt. She continued to pull at her leash, and I continued to hold on. She dragged me about four or five feet, my legs flailing behind me, through the rocks and desert grit. The retriever finally passed us, its owner shouting horrified apologies back over his shoulder, and my dog finally eased up. I took a deep breath and pulled myself to my feet. My knees were shaking. My shins were bloodied. My husband came rushing to me, apologizing that he had been unable to assist, since he had our other large dog on a leash and needed to stay out of the fray.

"Well, that was embarrassing," I finally managed to say, looking around for witnesses, my voice breaking, tears welling in my eyes.

"No," my husband said with a huge grin. "That was awesome! I'm so proud of you. You held on."

Had I let go, we might have had a dog fight on our hands. Had I let go, our girl might have run away into the desert. Rattle snakes, dehydration, and the busy highway were just a few of the dangers she would have faced. I had no choice but to hold on.

Writing a novel is like *that* walk in the park. Or, at least, it is for me. I have stories I desperately want to share, and so I have to hold on. I have to risk a little embarrassment, risk getting a little bloodied, to get the job done.

We went through a lot of dog training classes after that fateful day on the desert trail. But my girl was still unruly at times. Sure, we could have taken her to back to the rescue shelter, given up on her in favor of an easier dog, one more manageable. But she was part of the family. When she dropped her tattered sock-toy in my lap and patiently waited for me to throw it – her helicopter tail whirling, her big brown eyes dancing – I could only imagine the heartache I'd have felt if we had given up on her.

I've been through a lot of training myself since I started writing my first novel, despite my previous experience and success writing nonfiction. Multiples drafts, critiques, revisions, queries, and rejections were part of the long process leading to a polished manuscript and a publishing contract.

The story in that novel was a challenging, emotional, sometimes painful one to research and write. Sure, I could have put it in a drawer, given it up in favor of something easier to write. But the gratification of telling Margaret Morgan's story in a way that might touch or inspire those who read the book made all the hard work worthwhile. When the UPS truck pulled up to my house with a box full of books – fresh from the printer, with crisp pages and *All Different Kinds of Free* emblazoned on the glossy cover – I could only imagine the heartache I'd have felt if I had given up my quest to tell Margaret's story.

Whether you dream of writing a novel or of some other goal, my advice is to go for a walk in the park and hold on for the ride. Life is only half-lived if you haven't bloodied your knees at least a couple times.

Leveraging Rejection

> "The key to success is for you to make a habit throughout your life of doing the things you fear."
> – Vincent van Gogh, Dutch painter

"That's nice, dear, but don't let your voice overpower the others. Really, just a whisper is enough."

Those were not the words of a choir teacher stirred by the voice of her pupil, and their uninspired tone was not lost on an impressionable fifth grader.

To be fair, it really began years before that, with my brother in the back seat of the family Chevette. "Shut up!" he would demand as I crooned along with Karen Carpenter or Harry Chapin on the radio. Then he'd pound me. My parents, to spare me from a near-daily shellacking (and, I suspect, to spare themselves from my heartfelt renditions of "Close to You" and "Cat in the Cradle"), came up with a brilliant compromise. "It's a small car. Why don't you just lip-sync."

I continued to sing, with defiance and with heart and with emotion — and without making one audible sound. In the car, around the house, even in the choir, until my choir teacher finally suggested it was time for me to "try something different." Like soccer.

They were right. I can't sing. Whether it's because I was born with faulty pipes or because I was traumatized as a kid, I'll never know. For decades, I would break into cold sweats at little kids' birthday parties, get cotton mouth when the National Anthem played at the ball park, and whisper hymns at church. Karaoke? Not on your life.

But when I'm alone, my voice rings out loud and proud. Behind the wheel of my car, with the windows tightly shut and the radio cranked, I sing — with heart and with emotion and with sound. Music by Pat

Benatar, Alanis Morissette, and Pink inspire me — voices with depth and intensity, rebellion; lyrics with insight and meaning, attitude. They invite me to sing along, and I do, unabashedly.

When my daughter was born, I began singing soft lullabies, in the wee hours of the morning, when exhaustion and desperation had a will of its own. Hello, old friends, Karen, Harry. And, with a tiny baby in the backseat, my voice continued to ring out, uninhibited, in the car. Until, one day, another voice rang out sweetly. "Pretty, Mommy."

Amazing what the tiniest encouragement can do.

I still get jitters at birthday parties and ball games. But, if the crowd is big enough and loud enough, one more voice courageously joins the chorus. Just a whisper is no longer enough for me. Who knows, maybe one day I'll even sing Karaoke at my daughter's wedding.

And what of my writing?

One needs skin thick as whale blubber to survive this career. Author Bret Lott summed it up when he said,

"One thing I know most intimately and most truly about the life of a writer: You will be rejected. Period."

An aspiring writer I spoke to recently gasped when I told her how many agents I had queried for representation of my first novel. I wrote to more than fifty. I was rejected by forty-nine. My second novel generated similar numbers from agents and publishers. Rather than focusing on the dozens of polite no-thank-yous (and the handful of snarky no-ways), I clung to a few tiny encouragements contained within all those rejections: found much to admire in these pages; you write with a keen eye for detail; and, was crying at the end.

One publisher I queried had responded *Peculiar Savage Beauty* was "monotonous and lacking drama." Ouch.

Two years later, a *Publishers Weekly* review described the exact same manuscript as an atmospheric novel with a suspenseful plot.

The good news is that history is rife with stories of authors who were rejected – many of them multiple times and with gusto – and later achieve great success.

Such rejections have become things of legend, of absurdity, and are often printed in their entirety to shame long-dead editors for their unfortunate errors. Canadian arts and opinion magazine *Maisonneuve* recently published rejection letters sent to Virginia Woolf and Earnest Hemingway.

The Stanchion Press Editor David Balzer rejected Woolf's *To The Lighthouse* in 1926, writing, "I believe strongly in the old axiom of showing and not telling, but, in this case, I feel you do neither."[19] As for Hemingway's *The Sun Also Rises*, it was soundly rejected in 1925 by Peacock & Peacock Editor Moberley Luger, who found Hemingway's writing "to be both tedious and offensive."[20]

Contemporary authors have suffered the same treatment. Stephen King was rejected by thirty book publishers before Doubleday offered up a contract for *Carrie* in 1974. In the anthology *The Best Advice I Ever Got: Lessons from Extraordinary Lives,* Kathryn Stockett's essay revealed her long, painful path of rejection in seeking an agent for her manuscript.[21]

"[After] three and a half years of rejection, an agent named Susan Ramer took pity on me. In the end, I received sixty rejections for *The Help*. But letter number sixty-one was the one that accepted me," Stockett shared. "Three weeks later, Susan sold *The Help* to Amy Einhorn Books."

Published in 2009, Stockett's novel sold millions of copies, remained on the *New York Times* bestseller list for more than two years, and was made into an award-winning movie.

The end result of rejection is rarely that dramatic. For the vast majority of writers, success will come in small packages – an essay published in magazine, perhaps, or a modest book contract with an indie press. But to get there, rejections may number in the hundreds; and even after you've been published, the rejections and criticism will continue. It's just part of the business.

Career writers embrace every single rejection – regardless of how much they may sting – and learn from them. Often, even the most painful critique contains a small nugget of helpful information.

There will always be people in your life who will say you can't, you're not good enough. There will also be people who will offer encouraging words – yes, perhaps you can. Focus on the encouragers. Maybe your loudest, meanest critic is the one inside your head – the voice that says you can't, you're not good enough. We all have that voice.

Focus on the encouragers. You may not always find the specific success you chase, but you will find success and happiness when you ignore those negative voices.

Sing anyway.

Write anyway.

Do whatever it is you want to do anyway.

– The End –

"It is not the critic who counts…
The credit belongs to the man who is
actually in the arena, whose face is marred
by dust and sweat and blood, who strives
valiantly, who errs and comes up short
again and again… Who, at the worst, if he
fails, at least he fails while daring greatly."

– President Theodore Roosevelt,
American politician, conservationist,
and writer

Acknowledgments

My appreciation goes to the many people who suggested the idea and encouraged me to assemble a book about my life as a reader and writer. Such support has been an ongoing blessing throughout my career and personal journey. I hope *WORDS* holds up to your expectations. I'm grateful for all the editors and freelance clients who have appreciated my writing abilities and who enabled me to earn a living from my writing. Thanks to Tobi McCann for contributing her editing and proofreading talent to this work. Finally, thanks always go to my husband, Mike, for his unending encouragement and cheerleading.

Recommended Reading

> "There is no one so grateful as the man to whom you have given just the book his soul needed and he never knew it."
> – Christopher Morley, American novelist

In no particular order, the following is a list of books that I've read and have stayed with me. Many contain a story or an idea I needed to read at the exact time in life I read it. Some were just plain fun. Several made me a better writer. A few made me a better person.

Fiction

The Women in the Castle by Jessica Shattuck
All That is Solid Melts into Air by Darragh McKeon
The Orchardist by Amanda Coplin
A Gentleman in Moscow by Amor Towles
The Invisible Mountain by Carolina De Robertis

The Snow Child by Eowyn Ivey
Pictures of You by Caroline Leavitt
News of the World by Paulette Jiles
Of Mice and Men by John Steinbeck
The Night Circus by Erin Morgenstern
Dog on It (A Chet & Bernie Mystery) by Spencer Quinn
Winnie the Pooh by A.A. Milne
The Call of the Wild by Jack London
The Velveteen Rabbit by Margery Williams
A Hundred Small Lessons by Ashley Hay
The Story of Beautiful Girl by Rachel Simon

Nonfiction (general, memoir, writing)

Atomic Habits: An Easy & Proven Way to Build Good Habits & Break Bad Ones by James Clear
The Artist's Way, A Spiritual Path to Higher Creativity by Julia Cameron
The Power of Meaning, Finding Fulfillment in a World Obsessed with Happiness by Emily Esfahani Smith
Start. Punch Fear in the Face by Jon Acuff
Finish. Give Yourself the Gift of Done, by Jon Acuff

The Liar's Club by Mary Karr

Born on a Blue Day, Inside the Extraordinary Mind of an Autistic Savant by Daniel Tammet

365 Thank Yous, The Year a Simple Act of Daily Gratitude Changed My Life by John Kralik

On Writing, A Memoir of the Craft by Stephen King

Wild Mind, Living the Writer's Life by Natalie Goldberg

The Art of Memoir by Mary Karr

Writing Resources

Books

Wired for Story, The Writer's Guide to Using Brain Science to Hook Readers from the Very First Sentence by Lisa Cron

Word Work, Surviving and Thriving as a Writer by Bruce Holland Rogers

The Emotion Thesaurus: A Writer's Guide to Character Expression by Angela Ackerman and Becca Puglisi

The Elements of Style by William Strunk Jr. and E.B. White

American Popular Culture Through History: This series of books, from Greenwood Publishing Group, explores the activities, common items, popular opinions, entertainment, shopping habits, and other everyday aspects that impacted American life. Each volume focuses on a decade, from 1900 through 2000.

Online (free)

- *New York Times* archives (1851 to present)
  http://www.nytimes.com/ref/membercent
  er/nytarchive.html

- U.S. newspaper archives (1690 to present)
  http://chroniclingamerica.loc.gov/

- International newspaper archives
  http://www.loc.gov/rr/news/oltitles.html#forn

- Visual Color Thesaurus
  https://ingridsundberg.com/2014/02/04/the-color-
  thesaurus/

- Free historical image archive, Library of Congress
  https://www.loc.gov/free-to-use/

- *Saturday Evening Post* archives
  http://www.saturdayeveningpost.com/sections/
  archives

- Historical societies and organizations
  http://www.historians.org/affiliates/index.cfm

- Living history, farm and agricultural museums
  https://alhfam.org/museum-links

- Early Modern Resources (resources for years 1500-1800 and a wide range of topics)
  http://earlymodernweb.org/

- Historic city maps
  http://historic-cities.huji.ac.il/

- Popular baby names in United States by decade
  http://www.ssa.gov/oact/babynames/decades/index.html

- Sporting history
  https://historicalnovelsociety.org/sporting-history-resources-for-historical-fiction-writers/

- Food history
  http://foodmuseum.com/

Endnotes

1. Stillman, Jessica. "New Study: Reading Fiction Really Will Make You Nicer and More Empathetic." *Inc.Com*, 19 Feb. 2019, www.inc.com/jessica-stillman/reading-fiction-really-will-make-you-nicer-more-empathetic-new-study-says.html

2. Austin, Michael. "Want a Better Life? Read a Book." *Pyschologytoday.Com*, 15 Mar. 2012, www.psychologytoday.com/us/blog/ethics-everyone/201203/want-better-life-read-book

3. Maass, Donald. *Writing the Breakout Novel*. F+W Media, 2002.

4. Fryxell, David. *How to Write Fast (While Writing Well)*. Writer's Digest Books, 1995.

5. Rogers, Bruce Holland. *Word Work: Surviving and Thriving As a Writer*. 1st ed., Invisible Cities Press LLC, 2002.

6. Cameron, Julia. *The Artist's Way: A Spiritual Path to Higher Creativity*. Jeremy P. Tarcher/Perigee, 1992.

7. "One Man's Dream 2010" *YouTube*, sand art uploaded by Ilana Yahav, 31 Dec. 2009, https://youtu.be/dEgSoTCgvgA

8. Cron, Lisa. *Wired for Story: The Writer's Guide to Using Brain Science to Hook Readers from the Very First Sentence*. Ten Speed Press, 2012.

9. Doctorow, E. L. *Ragtime*. Penguin Classics, 1974.

10. Maass, Donald. *Writing the Breakout Novel*. F+W Media, 2002.

11. Rogers, Bruce Holland. *Word Work: Surviving and Thriving As a Writer*. 1st ed., Invisible Cities Press LLC, 2002.

12. Clear, James. *Atomic Habits: An Easy & Proven Way to Build Good Habits & Break Bad Ones*. Penguin Random House, 2018.

13. Chamblee Carpenter, Dana. "Writing with Wonder: Weaving Time and Place with Story in Historical Fiction." *Writersdigest.Com*, 10 Oct. 2018, www.writersdigest.com/editor-blogs/questions-and-quandaries/writing-advice/writing-with-wonder-weaving-time-and-place-with-story-in-historical-fiction

14. Woolley, Persia. *How to Write and Sell Historical Fiction*. F+W Media, 1997.

15. Masashi, Soga. "Gardening Is Beneficial for Health: A Meta-Analysis." National Center for Biotechnology Information, *Preventive Medicine Reports*, 1 Mar. 2017, www.ncbi.nlm.nih.gov/pmc/articles/PMC5153451

16. Louv, Richard. *Last Child in the Woods: Saving Our Children from Nature-Deficit Disorder*. Algonquin Books, 2008.

17. Louv, Richard. *The Nature Principle: Reconnecting with Life in a Virtual Age*. Algonquin Books, 2012.

18. Loh KK, Kanai R (2014) Higher Media Multi-Tasking Activity Is Associated with Smaller Gray-Matter Density in the Anterior Cingulate Cortex. PLoS ONE 9(9): e106698.

19. Balzer, David. "Virginia Woolf's Lost Rejection Letter." *Maisonneuve*, 13 May 2005, maisonneuve.org/article/2005/05/13/virginia-woolfs-lost-rejection-letter

20. Luger, Moberley. "Ernest Hemingway's Lost Rejection Letter." *Maisonneuve*, 13 May 2005, maisonneuve.org/article/2005/05/13/ernest-hemingways-lost-rejection-letter

21. Stockett, Kathryn. (Essay). *The Best Advice I Ever Got: Lessons from Extraordinary Lives*, edited by Katie Couric, Random House Publishing Group, 2012.